SCIENTOLOGY

Making the World a Better P|

MW01248665

Founded and developed by L. Ron Hubbard, Scientology is an applied religious philosophy which offers an exact route through which anyone can regain the truth and simplicity of his spiritual self.

Scientology consists of specific axioms that define the underlying causes and principles of existence and a vast area of observations in the humanities, a philosophic body that literally applies to the entirety of life.

This broad body of knowledge resulted in two applications of the subject: first, a technology for man to increase his spiritual awareness and attain the freedom sought by many great philosophic teachings; and, second, a great number of fundamental principles men can use to improve their lives. In fact, in this second application, Scientology offers nothing less than practical methods to better *every* aspect of our existence—means to create new ways of life. And from this comes the subject matter you are about to read.

Compiled from the writings of L. Ron Hubbard, the data presented here is but one of the tools which can be found in *The Scientology Handbook*. A comprehensive guide, the handbook contains numerous applications of Scientology which can be used to improve many other areas of life.

In this booklet, the editors have augmented the data with a short introduction, practical exercises and examples of successful application.

Courses to increase your understanding and further materials to broaden your knowledge are available at your nearest Scientology church or mission, listed at the back of this booklet.

Many new phenomena about man and life are described in Scientology, and so you may encounter terms in these pages you are not familiar with. These are described the first time they appear and in the glossary at the back of the booklet.

Scientology is for use. It is a practical philosophy, something one *does*. Using this data, you *can* change conditions.

Millions of people who want to do something about the conditions they see around them have applied this knowledge. They know that life can be improved. And they know that Scientology works.

Use what you read in these pages to help yourself and others and you will too.

CHURCH OF SCIENTOLOGY INTERNATIONAL

A man is as alive as he can communicate," L. Ron Hubbard wrote. And communication is a facet of life which he explored very deeply indeed, ultimately writing hundreds of thousands of words about this vital subject. Communication skills are essential in **any** sphere of human interaction. In fact, when all is said and done, on whatever level, communication is the sole activity all people share.

The benefits of effective communication are too numerous to list, for they enhance all aspects of life from the personal to the professional. The **ability** to communicate is vital to the success of any endeavor.

In this booklet you will learn what good communication consists of and how to recognize the bad, what the component parts of communication are and how to utilize them, and why more communication, not less, brings the individual greater freedom.

Also included in this booklet are numerous drills that Mr. Hubbard developed which improve one's communication level and have great practical application to life. A thorough understanding of this data will provide you with tools you can use forever. ■

WHAT IS COMMUNICATION?

How does one talk so that another person listens and understands? How does one listen? How does one know if he has been heard and understood?

These are all points about communication that have never before been analyzed or explained.

People have known that communication is an important part of life but until now no one has ever been able to tell anyone *how* to communicate.

Until Scientology, the subject of communication had received no emphasis or study. Any attention given to it was mechanical and the province of engineers. Yet all human endeavor depends utterly on a full knowledge of the real basics of communication.

To master communication, one must understand it.

In Scientology, communication *has* been defined—an accomplishment that has led to a much deeper understanding of life itself.

Communication, in essence, is the shift of a particle from one part of space to another part of space. A *particle* is the thing being communicated. It can be an object, a written message, a spoken word or an idea. In its crudest definition, this *is* communication.

This simple view of communication leads to the full definition:

Communication is the consideration and action of impelling an impulse or particle from source-point across a distance to receipt-point, with the intention of bringing into being at the receipt-point a duplication and understanding of that which emanated from the source-point.

Duplication is the act of reproducing something exactly. *Emanated* means "came forth."

The formula of communication is cause, distance, effect, with intention, attention and duplication *with understanding.*

The definition and formula of communication open the door to understanding this subject. By dissecting communication into its component parts, we can view the function of each and thus more clearly understand the whole.

Any communication involves a particle which can be in one of four categories: an object…

…a written message…

…a spoken word…

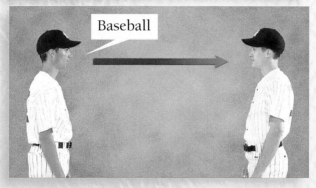

…or an idea.

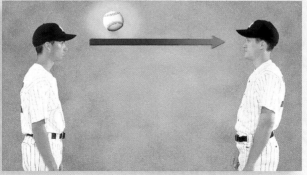

**DUPLICATION
AND
UNDERSTANDING**

Receipt-Point

Any successful communication contains all the elements shown here. Any failure to communicate can be analyzed against these components to isolate what went wrong.

FACTORS OF COMMUNICATION

Let us now more closely examine several components of communication by looking at two life units, one of them "A" and the other "B." "A" and "B" are terminals—by terminal we mean a point that receives, relays and sends communication.

First there is "A's" *intention*. This, at "B" becomes *attention,* and for a true communication to take place, a *duplication* at "B" must take place of what emanated from "A."

"A" of course, to emanate a communication, must have given attention originally to "B," and "B" must have given to this communication some intention, at least to listen or receive, so we have both cause and effect having intention and attention.

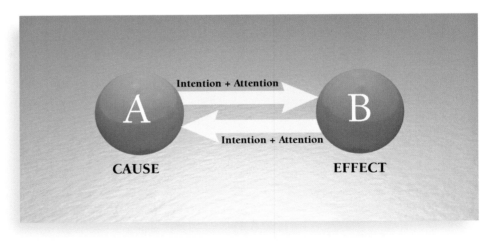

Now, there is another factor which is very important. This is the factor of duplication. We could express this as reality, or we could express it as agreement. The degree of agreement reached between "A" and "B" in this communication cycle becomes their reality, and this is accomplished mechanically by duplication. In other words, the degree of reality reached in this communication cycle depends upon the amount of duplication. "B" as effect, must to some degree duplicate what emanated from "A" as cause, in order for the first part of the cycle to take effect.

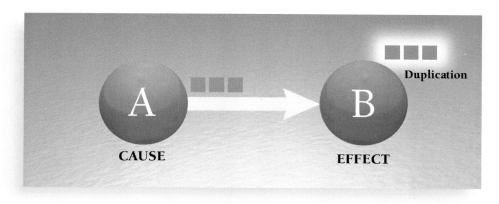

Then "A," now as effect, must duplicate what emanated from "B" for the communication to be concluded. If this is done there is no detrimental consequence.

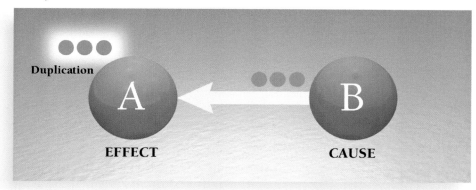

If this duplication does not take place at "B" and then at "A" we get what amounts to an unfinished cycle of action. If, for instance, "B" did not vaguely duplicate what emanated from "A," the first part of the cycle of communication was not achieved, and a great deal of randomity (unpredicted motion), explanation, argument might result. Then if "A" did not duplicate what emanated from "B" when "B" was cause on the second cycle, again an uncompleted cycle of communication occurred with consequent unreality. Now naturally, if we cut down reality, we will cut down affinity—the feeling of love or liking for something or someone. So, where duplication is absent, affinity is seen to drop.

A complete cycle of communication will result in high affinity. If we disarrange any of these factors we get an incomplete cycle of communication and we have either "A" or "B" or both *waiting* for the end of cycle. In such a wise the communication becomes harmful.

An unfinished cycle of communication generates what might be called *answer hunger.* An individual who is waiting for a signal that his communication has been received is prone to accept any inflow. When an individual has, for a very long period of time, consistently waited for answers which did not arrive, any sort of answer from anywhere will be pulled in to him, by him, as an effort to remedy his scarcity for answers.

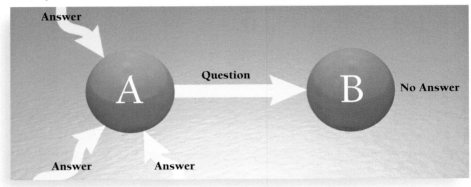

Uncompleted cycles of communication bring about a scarcity of answers. It does not much matter what the answers were or would be as long as they vaguely approximate the subject at hand. It does matter when some entirely unlooked-for answer is given, as in compulsive or obsessive communication, or when no answer is given at all.

Communication itself is detrimental only when the emanating communication at cause was sudden and non sequitur (illogical) to the environment. Here we have violations of attention and intention.

The factor of interest also enters here but is far less important. Nevertheless, it explains a great deal about human behavior. "A" has the intention of interesting "B." "B," to be talked to, becomes interesting.

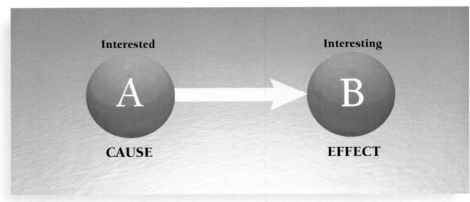

Similarly "B," when he emanates a communication, is interest*ed* and "A" is interest*ing*.

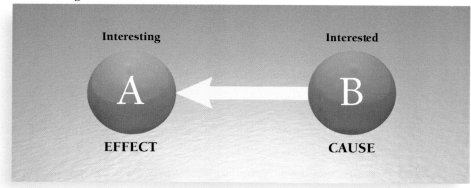

Here we have, as part of the communication formula (but a less important part), the continuous shift from being interested to being interesting on the part of either of the terminals, "A" or "B." Cause is interest*ed,* effect is interest*ing.*

Of some greater importance is the fact that the intention to be received on the part of "A" places upon "A" the necessity of being duplicatable.

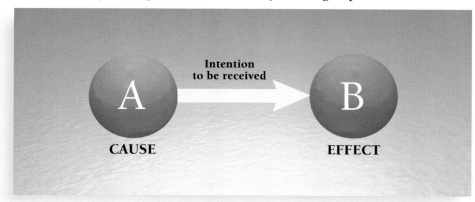

If "A" cannot be duplicatable in any degree, then of course his communication will not be received at "B," for "B," unable to duplicate "A," cannot receive the communication.

As an example of this, "A," let us say, speaks in Chinese, where "B" can only understand French. It is necessary for "A" to make himself duplicatable by speaking French to "B" who only understands French. In a case where "A" speaks one language and "B" another, and they have no language in common, we have the factor of mimicry possible and a communication can yet take place. "A," supposing he had a hand, could raise his hand. "B," supposing he had one, could raise his hand. Then "B" could raise his other hand, and "A" could raise his other hand, and we would have completed a cycle of communication by mimicry.

Basically, all things are considerations. We consider that things are, and so they are. The idea is always senior to the mechanics of energy, space, time, mass. It would be possible to have entirely different ideas about communication than these. However, these happen to be the ideas of communication which are in common in this universe, and which are utilized by the life units of this universe.

Here we have the basic agreement upon the subject of communication in the communication formula as given here. Because ideas are senior to this, a being can get, in addition to the communication formula, a peculiar idea concerning just exactly how communication should be conducted, and if this is not generally agreed upon, can find himself definitely out of communication.

Let us take the example of a modernistic writer who insists that the first three letters of every word should be dropped or that no sentence should be finished. He will not attain agreement among his readers.

There is a continuous action of natural selection, one might say, which weeds out strange or peculiar communication ideas. People, to be in communication, adhere to the basic rules as given here, and when anyone tries to depart too widely from these rules, they simply do not duplicate him and so, in effect, he goes out of communication.

Now we come to the problem of what a life unit must be willing to experience in order to communicate. In the first place the primary source-point must be willing to be duplicatable. It must be able to give at least some attention to the receipt-point. The primary receipt-point must be willing to duplicate,

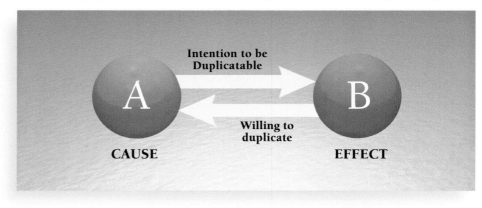

must be willing to receive and must be willing to change into a source-point in order to send the communication, or an answer to it, back. And the primary source-point in its turn must be willing to be a receipt-point.

As we are dealing basically with ideas and not mechanics, we see, then, that a state of mind must exist between a cause- and effect-point whereby each one is willing to be cause or effect at will, is willing to duplicate at will, is willing to be duplicatable at will, is willing to change at will, is willing to experience the distance between, and, in short, willing to communicate.

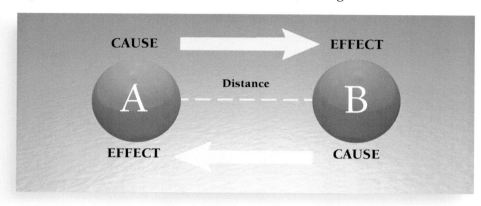

Where we get these conditions in an individual or a group we have sane people.

Where an unwillingness to send or receive communications occurs, where people obsessively or compulsively send communications without direction and without trying to be duplicatable, where individuals in receipt of communications stand silent and do not acknowledge or reply, we have factors of irrationality.

Some of the conditions which can occur in an irrational line are a failure to be duplicatable before one emanates a communication, an intention contrary to being received, an unwillingness to receive or duplicate a communication, an unwillingness to experience distance, an unwillingness to change, an unwillingness to give attention, an unwillingness to express intention, an unwillingness to acknowledge, and, in general, an unwillingness to duplicate.

It might be seen by someone that the solution to communication is not to communicate. One might say that if he hadn't communicated in the first place he wouldn't be in trouble now. Perhaps there is some truth in this, but a man is as dead as he can't communicate. He is as alive as he can communicate.

TWO-WAY COMMUNICATION

A cycle of communication and two-way communication are actually two different things. If we examine closely the anatomy of communication—the actual structure and parts—we will discover that a cycle of communication is not a two-way communication in its entirety.

If you will inspect Graph A below, you will see a cycle of communication:

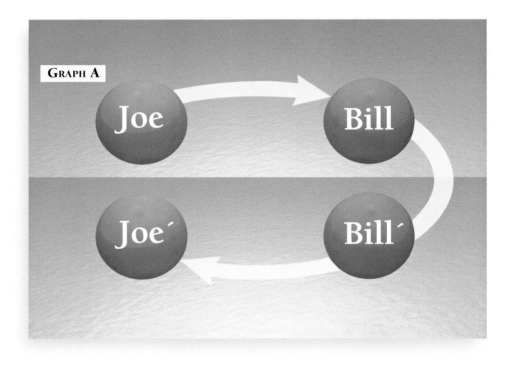

GRAPH A

Here we have Joe as the originator of a communication. It is his primary impulse. This impulse is addressed to Bill. We find Bill receiving it, and then Bill originating an answer or acknowledgment as Bill´, which acknowledgment is sent back to Joe´. Joe has said, for instance, "How are you?" Bill has received this, and then Bill (becoming secondary cause) has replied to it as Bill´ with "I'm okay," which goes back to Joe´ and thus ends the cycle.

Now what we call a two-way cycle of communication may ensue as in Graph B below:

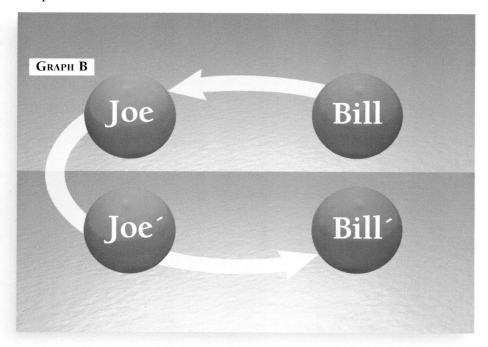

Here we have Bill originating a communication. Bill says, "How's tricks?" Joe receives this, and then as Joe´ or secondary cause, answers "Okay, I guess," which answer is then acknowledged in its receipt by Bill´.

In both of these graphs we discover that in Graph A the acknowledgment of the secondary cause was expressed by Joe´ as a nod or a look of satisfaction. And again, in Graph B Joe´'s "Okay, I guess" is actually acknowledged by Bill´ with a nod or some expression signifying the receipt of the communication.

If both Joe and Bill are "strong, silent men," they would omit some portion of these cycles. The most flagrant omission and the one most often understood as "communication lag" would be for Joe in Graph A to say, "How are you?" and for Bill to stand there without speaking. (By "communication lag" is meant the length of time intervening between the asking of a question and the reply to that specific question by the person asked.)

Here we have Joe causing a communication, and Bill´ failing to continue the cycle. We do not know or inquire, and we are not interested in, whether or not Bill as the receipt-point ever did hear it. We can assume that he was at least present, and that Joe spoke loudly enough to be heard, and that Bill's attention was somewhere in Joe's vicinity. Now, instead of getting on with the cycle of communication, Joe is left there with an incompleted cycle and never gets an opportunity to become Joe´.

There are several ways in which a cycle of communication could not be completed, and these could be categorized as:

1. Joe failing to emanate a communication,

2. Bill failing to hear the communication,

3. Bill´ failing to reply to the communication received by him, and

4. Joe´ failing to acknowledge by some sign or word that he has heard Bill´.

We could assign various reasons to all this, but our purpose here is not to assign reasons why they do not complete a communication cycle. Our entire purpose is involved with the noncompletion of this communication cycle.

Now, as in Graph A, let us say we have in Joe a person who is compulsively and continually originating communications whether he has anybody's attention or not, and whether or not these communications are germane (pertinent) to any existing situation. We discover that Joe is apt to be met, in his communicating, with an inattentive Bill who does not hear him, and thus an absent Bill´ who does not answer him, and thus an absent Joe´ who never acknowledges.

Let us examine this same situation in Graph B. Here we have, in Bill, an origination of a communication. We have the same Joe with a compulsive outflow. Bill says, "How are you?" and the cycle is not completed because Joe, so intent upon his own compulsive line, does not become Joe´ and never gives Bill a chance to become Bill´ and acknowledge.

Now let us take another situation. We find Joe originating communications, and Bill a person who never originates communications. Joe is not necessarily compulsive or obsessive in originating communications, but Bill is inhibited in originating communications. We find that Joe and Bill, working together, then get into this kind of an activity: Joe originates communication, Bill hears it, becomes Bill´, replies to it, and permits Joe a chance to become Joe´. This goes on quite well, but will sooner or later hit a jam on a two-way cycle, which is violated because Bill never originates communication.

A two-way cycle of communication would work as follows: Joe, having originated a communication and having completed it, may then wait for Bill to originate a communication to Joe, thus completing the remainder of the two-way cycle of communication. Bill does originate a communication, this is heard by Joe, answered by Joe´ and acknowledged by Bill´.

Thus we get the normal cycle of a communication between two terminals, for in this case Joe is a terminal and Bill is a terminal and communication can be seen to flow between two terminals. The cycles depend on Joe originating communication, Bill hearing the communication, Bill becoming Bill´ and answering the communication, Joe´ acknowledging the communication, then Bill originating a communication, Joe hearing the communication, Joe´ answering the communication and Bill´ acknowledging the communication.

If they did this, regardless of what they were talking about, they would never become in an argument and would eventually reach an agreement, even if they were hostile to one another. Their difficulties and problems would be cleared up and they would be, in relationship to each other, in good shape.

A two-way communication cycle breaks down when either terminal fails, in its turn, to originate communications. We discover that the entire society has vast difficulties along this line. They are so used to canned entertainment and so inhibited in originating communications by parents who couldn't communicate, and by education and other causes, that people get very low on communication origin. Communication origin is necessary to start a communication in the first place.

Thus we find people talking mainly about things which are forced upon them by exterior causes. They see an accident, they discuss it. They see a movie, they discuss it. They wait for an exterior source to give them the occasion for a conversation. But in view of the fact that both are low on the origin of communication—which could also be stated as low on imagination—we discover that such people, dependent on exterior primal impulses, are more or less compulsive or inhibitive in communication, and thus the conversation veers rapidly and markedly and may wind up with some remarkable animosities (hostile feelings) or misconclusions.

Let us suppose that lack of prime or original cause impulse on Joe's part has brought him into obsessive or compulsive communication, and we find that he is so busy outflowing that he never has a chance to hear anyone who speaks to him, and if he did hear them, would not answer them. Bill, on the other hand, might be so very, very, very low on primal cause (which is to say, low on communication origination) that he never even moves into Bill´, or if he does, would never put forth his own opinion, thus unbalancing Joe further and further into further and further compulsive communication.

As you can see by these graphs, some novel situations could originate. There would be the matter of obsessive answering as well as inhibitive answering. An individual could spend all of his time answering, justifying or explaining—all the same thing—no primal communication having been originated at him. Another individual, as Joe´ in Graph A or Bill´ in Graph B, might spend all of his time acknowledging, even though nothing came his way to acknowledge. The common and most noticed manifestations, however, are obsessive and compulsive origin, and nonanswering acceptance, and nonacknowledgment of answer. And at these places we can discover stuck flows.

As the only crime in the universe seems to be to communicate, and as the only saving grace of a person is to communicate, we can readily understand that an entanglement of communication is certain to result. What we should understand—and much more happily—is that it can now be resolved.

Flows become stuck on this twin cycle of communication where a scarcity occurs in:

1. origination of communication,

2. receipt of communication,

3. answering a communication given,

4. acknowledging answers.

Thus it can be seen that there are only four parts which can become problematic in both Graph A and Graph B, no matter the number of peculiar manifestations which can occur as a result thereof.

COMMUNICATION TRAINING DRILLS

Now that you have discovered the component parts of communication and its formula, how do you use this knowledge? How do you put into practice what you have just studied on the formula of communication? How do you apply the laws of communication so easily and naturally that they almost seem to be a part of you? How, in fact, do you become effective in communication?

In Scientology there are drills that enable anyone to improve his or her level of communication skill. A *drill* is a method of learning or training whereby a person does a procedure over and over again in order to perfect that skill. These communication drills, called *Training Routines* or *TRs* for short, deal with the various parts of the communication formula.

The TRs were originally developed to train Scientology practitioners in technical application, as a high level of communication skill is vital for this activity. However, by drilling each part of the communication formula with these TRs, *any* person's ability to master the communication cycle and thus better communicate with others can be vastly improved.

By doing these drills you will learn how to make your communication understood by others and how to truly understand what they say to you, how to be what is sometimes called "a good listener," how to guide a communication cycle you are having with another person and how to recognize and rectify failures in the communication cycles of others.

These are all skills of immeasurable value in day-to-day life. No matter what your occupation or what kind of activities you are involved in, the ability to communicate with ease and certainty is essential.

The TRs cannot be done alone; you must do them with the help of another person. The way that this is done is that you pair up with another person and do the drills together. This is done on a turnabout basis: when you are doing the drill, the other person helps you become skilled on that drill. Then you switch around and help the other person while he or she does the drill. The action of helping another through the drill is called *coaching*.

The drills give directions for the roles of *student* and *coach*. When you are practicing the drill you are called the *student,* and the person helping you get through the drill is called the *coach*.

It makes no difference whether you start out first as student and your partner as coach, or vice versa. You both take turns being student then coach, to get each other through the drills. By helping each other through the TRs on this alternating basis, you are both able to learn how to fully use the communication cycle.

So, before you embark on doing the TRs, find another person to do the drills with you on this turnabout basis of *student* and *coach*.

It is very important that both you and your partner read through and understand all these drills *before* beginning to practice them. Also, another section follows the drills which explains how to coach someone correctly. This too should be thoroughly studied and understood before the drills are started, as coaching is a very precise procedure. It is vital that proper coaching is done in order to achieve the best possible gains from the TRs.

Each of the TRs has a *Number* and a *Name,* which are simply designations to refer to them by.

The *Commands* are the spoken directions used in starting, continuing and stopping the drill in coaching, and the questions or statements used while doing the TR.

Each drill also states the *Position* you are to sit in.

The particular communication skill that you are aiming to achieve on each TR is stated under its *Purpose.*

The *Training Stress* outlines how that drill is to be done and gives the important points to stress or emphasize in coaching.

Patter is included in some of the drills to show how the various commands or questions are used during the procedure. In Scientology, the word *patter* simply means the special vocabulary of a drill.

When done diligently and exactly as written, these drills lead to successful communication—for anyone.

Do the following:

1. Read all the way through the drills on the following pages, as well as the section entitled *Coaching*.

2. Find someone to work with as a partner so you can get each other through the drills.

3. Have your partner read through all the drills and the section on *Coaching*.

4. Decide which of you will coach first.

5. Then start the first TR!

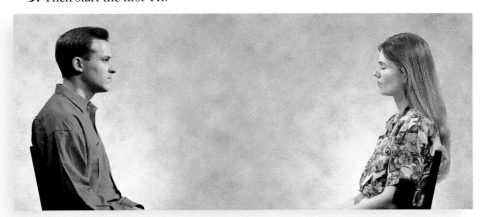

Number: TR 0 Be There

Name: Be There

Commands: The coach says "Start" to begin the drill. The coach uses "That's it" to end the drill or to point out an error to the student. Example: Student falls asleep; coach says, "That's it. You went to sleep. Start."

In this and all drills, when the student has achieved the purpose of the drill, the coach says, "Pass."

Although there is actually little coaching involved in this drill, some is required. The coach starts the drill and keeps the student at it until he passes.

Position: Student and coach sit facing each other a comfortable distance apart—about three feet. The student has his eyes closed.

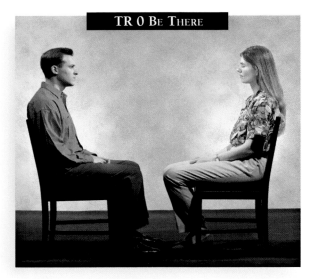

TR 0 BE THERE

Purpose: To train student to be there comfortably. The idea is to get the student able to *be* there comfortably in a position three feet in front of another person, to *be* there and not do anything else but *be* there.

In order to start a communication, you must be in a place from which to communicate. If you are not *there,* you will not be able to properly start a communication. Being there is a requisite to good communication; there is nothing more complex to it than that.

The student's eyes are closed in this drill to make it easy to be there, as the first step. With eyes closed, one does not have the added requirement of confronting another person, but can simply become accustomed to being there in a relaxed manner.

Training Stress: Student and coach sit facing each other. The student has his eyes closed. There is no conversation. This is a silent drill. There is *no* twitching, moving, "system" or methods used or anything else added to *be* there. Doing something with his body, or forcing his back against the chair in an effort to stay alert, are examples of systems or methods being used instead of simply being there.

One will usually see blackness or an area of the room when one's eyes are closed. *Be there comfortably.*

It is the task of the coach to keep the student alert and doing the drill.

Sit in an upright position in a straight-backed chair. Do the drill until there is no tendency or desire to squirm, twitch, move or change position. If such "turn on," then continue the drill until they are flattened. *Flattened* means the drill has been continued until it no longer produces a reaction.

The student is to do this drill until he is fully convinced, without reservations, that he can continue to sit quietly and comfortably for an indefinite period without any compulsion to twitch or shift about or having to repress such compulsions.

When he can *be* there comfortably and has reached a *major stable win,* the drill is passed.

People commonly experience many improvements while doing TRs, such as an improved ability to confront and to communicate, heightened perceptions, and so on. These are called *wins* as the student has desired to improve his communication skills and his awareness, and each achievement toward accomplishing that is itself a *win.* A *major stable win* means the student has reached the point where he can do that drill, and his skill and ability to do it is stable. A major stable win is a significant, lasting gain.

Number: TR 0 Confronting

Name: Confronting

Confronting is defined as being able to face. When we say one is confronting, we mean that he is facing without flinching or avoiding. The ability to confront is actually the ability to be there comfortably and perceive.

Commands: Coach: "Start," "That's it," "Flunk."

The coach has several terms he uses. The first of these is "Start," at which moment the drill begins. Every time the student does not hold his position, slumps, goes unconscious, twitches, starts his eyes wandering, or in any way demonstrates an incorrect position, the coach says "Flunk" and corrects the difficulty. He then says "Start" again and the drill goes on. When the coach wishes to make comments, he says "That's it," straightens up this point and then again says "Start."

Position: Student and coach sit facing each other a comfortable distance apart—about three feet. Both are looking at each other.

Purpose: To acquire the skill of being able to sit quietly and look at someone without strain.

This drill is the next level of skill up from *TR 0 Be There*. Now he must also confront.

Communication is not really possible in the absence of confront. Have you ever tried to talk to someone who won't look at you? That person is not confronting you. Lack of confront is a barrier to real communication.

Nervous twitches, tensions, all stem from an unwillingness to confront. When that willingness is repaired, these disabilities tend to disappear.

Training Stress: Student and coach sit facing each other, neither making any conversation or effort to be interesting. They sit and look at each other and say and do nothing for some hours. Student must not speak, fidget, giggle or be embarrassed or fall asleep.

It will be found the student tends to confront *with* a body part, rather than just confront. Confronting with a body part can cause the body part to hurt or feel uncomfortable. The solution is just to confront and be there.

The basic rule is that anything which the student is holding tense is the thing *with* which he is confronting. If the student's eyes begin to smart, he is confronting with them. If his stomach begins to protrude and becomes tense, he is confronting with his stomach. If his shoulders or even the back of his head become tense, then he is confronting with the shoulders or the back of his head. An expert coach would in this case give a "That's it," correct the student and then start the drill session anew.

A blink is not a flunk on TR 0 and "blinkless" is not a requirement. The coach should not put any attention on whether somebody is blinking—only on whether or not the person is confronting.

However, wide-eyed staring is unnatural and means the student is trying to confront with his eyes. In such a case the student's eyes will water, become red and will hurt if he continues. A student having excessive trouble with his eyes should be returned to *TR 0 Be There* and master this drill before again attempting to do *TR 0 Confronting*.

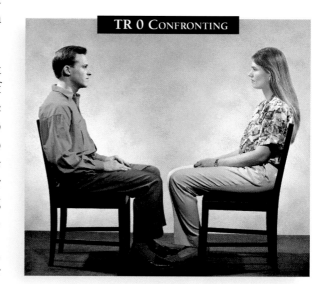

TR 0 CONFRONTING

As with *TR 0 Be There,* the student does not use any system or method of confronting other than just *be* there. The drill is misnamed if confronting means to *do* something. The whole action is to accustom the student to comfortably *be there* three feet in front of another without apologizing or moving or being startled or embarrassed or defending self.

Continue the drill until any twitches, flinches or other manifestations no longer exist or have to be suppressed (kept from being known or seen). Anything that turns on will flatten.

Student passes when he can just *be* there and confront and he has reached a *major stable win.*

Number: TR 0 Bullbait

Name: Confronting, Bullbaited

The term *bullbait* means to find certain actions, words, phrases, mannerisms or subjects that cause a student doing the drill to become distracted by reacting to the coach. The word *bullbait* is derived from an English and Spanish sport of *baiting* which meant to set dogs upon a chained bull.

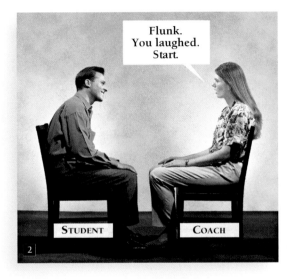

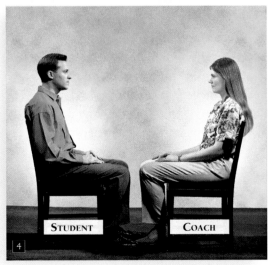

In the photographs above, the coach finds a button on the student (1) and flunks him for breaking his confront (2). She resumes the drill and repeats the phrase which made him react (3), repeating it until the student can comfortably confront it,

It will be found that people have certain things that cause them to react in some way. In Scientology we call this a *button*: an item, word, phrase, subject or area that causes response or reaction in an individual.

For example, the coach says something to the student like, "You have big ears." The student reacts by laughing uncontrollably. The coach has thus found a button on that student. This is bullbaiting.

Commands: Coach: "Start," "That's it," "Flunk."

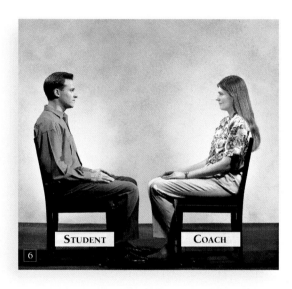

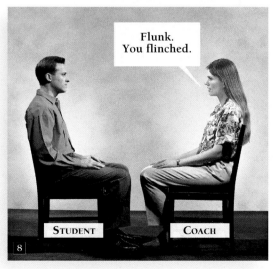

without reacting to it (4, 5, 6). She continues bullbaiting, trying to find another button. When she does so (7), she flunks the student with the reason why (8) and would now proceed to flatten the new button.

Position: Student and coach sit facing each other a comfortable distance apart—about three feet.

Purpose: To acquire the skill of being able to sit quietly and look at someone without strain and without being thrown off, distracted or made to react in any way to what the other person says or does.

In the previous drill, a student learns how to confront with the coach just sitting silently. In *TR 0 Bullbait* the student's ability to confront is increased further and he learns not to be thrown off by the actions of the coach.

This enhances the ability to be there and deliver a communication to another, in any social or life situation, without being distracted by anything.

For example, have you ever had the experience of talking to someone and becoming tongue-tied or flustered when the other person brought up some other subject? Have you ever reacted uncontrollably to something another said even though you didn't want to? This drill can increase your ability to be more causative and in control, in all aspects of communication.

Training Stress: After the student has passed *TR 0 Confronting* and can just *be* there comfortably, "bullbaiting" can begin. Anything added to *being there* is sharply flunked by the coach. Twitches, blinks, sighs, fidgets, anything except just being there is promptly flunked, with the reason why.

Patter as a Coach: Student coughs. Coach: "Flunk! You coughed. Start." This is the whole of the coach's patter as a coach.

Patter as a Confronted Subject: The coach may say anything or do anything except leave the chair. However, the coach must be realistic in his coaching, giving real conditions and circumstances that could come up in everyday life. The coach may not touch the student.

The student's buttons can be found and tromped on hard until they no longer produce a reaction. Any words not coaching words may receive *no* response from the student. If student responds, the coach is instantly a coach (and follows the patter above).

Student passes when he can *be* there comfortably without being thrown off or distracted or made to react in any way to anything the coach says or does and has reached a *major stable win*.

Number: TR 1

Name: Getting Your Communication Across

Purpose: To acquire the skill of getting one specific communication across to a listener and understood.

Have you ever seen someone who just keeps talking, without ever knowing whether or not his communications are being received? Making oneself understood is an important part of the communication formula.

Commands: A phrase (with the "he said's" omitted) is picked out of the book *Alice in Wonderland* and read to the coach. It is repeated until the coach is satisfied it arrived where he is.

Position: Student and coach are seated facing each other a comfortable distance apart.

Training Stress: The communication goes from the book to the student and, as his own, to the coach. It must not go from book to coach. It must sound natural not artificial. Diction (the manner of pronouncing words) and elocution (the mannerisms and art of public speaking) have no part in it. Loudness may have.

The coach must have received the communication (or question) clearly and have understood it before he says "Good."

There is no special significance to using the book *Alice in Wonderland*. In this drill you say things from a book instead of making them up.

Any idea is yours that you make yours. When you take an idea out of a book, it becomes your idea, and then as your idea you relay it to another person. The drill is coached this way. The communication is not from the book to the coach. It is from the book to the student, and then the student, making it his own idea, expresses that idea to the coach in such a way that it arrives at the coach.

We know at once a person can't communicate when he cannot take this first basic step of taking an idea, owning it and then communicating it to someone else.

In coaching we want the student to find a phrase in *Alice in Wonderland* and then, taking that as his own idea, communicate it directly to the coach. He can say the same phrase over and over, if he wishes, in any way he wishes to say it, until the coach tells him that he thinks the communication has arrived.

It is the intention that communicates, not the words. When the intention to communicate to a person goes across, the communication will arrive.

The intention must communicate, and it must be communicated in one unit of time. It isn't repeated from the last time it was repeated. It is new, fresh, communicated in present time. Once a communication is relayed across successfully, then he can find another communication and communicate that.

Patter: The coach says "Start," says "Good" without a new start if the communication is received or says "Flunk" if the communication is not received. "Start" is not used again. "That's it" is used to terminate for a discussion or to end the activity. If the drill session is terminated for a discussion, coach must say "Start" again before it resumes.

This drill is passed only when the student can put across a communication naturally, without strain or artificiality or elocutionary bobs and gestures, and when the student can do it easily and relaxedly.

Number: TR 2

Name: Acknowledgments

An *acknowledgment* is something said or done to inform another that his statement or action has been noted, understood and received.

Purpose: To acquire the skill of totally, completely and finally acknowledging a statement, observation or comment in such a way that the person making it is happy with the fact that it has been wholly received and understood and feels no need to repeat or continue it.

Acknowledgment is a control factor in the cycle of communication. This is true of any communication cycle in any type of situation. The formula of control is start, change and stop. If you can start something, change it and then stop it, you are in control of it. An acknowledgment is a "stop." Therefore, if one acknowledges the communications of others properly, he can control communication.

If you said to someone, "Keep going" or "Keep talking," you would not be acknowledging him. The perfect acknowledgment communicates only this: *I have heard your communication.* It signalizes that the person's communication to you has been received. It isn't the word that ends a cycle of communication, it's the intention that ends it.

TR 2

"I feel faint. Give me a ham sandwich."

COACH   STUDENT

"Right away."

COACH   STUDENT

In life, it is actually very therapeutic for a person to know that he has been acknowledged.

Commands: The coach reads lines from *Alice in Wonderland,* omitting the "he said's," and the student thoroughly acknowledges them. The student says "Good," "Fine," "Okay," "I heard that," *anything* only so long as it is appropriate to the person's communication—in such a way as actually to convince the person who is sitting there that he has heard it. The coach repeats any line he feels was not truly acknowledged.

Position: Student and coach are seated facing each other at a comfortable distance apart.

Training Stress: The student must acknowledge in such a way that the coach is convinced there is no need to repeat himself, that it has been received and understood, totally and finally.

The student does this by *intending* that the communication cycle ends at that point and ending it there. Anything the student does to make that come about is legitimate provided that it does not dismay or upset the coach. The student acknowledges in a manner appropriate to the coach's communication and convinces the coach that he has received it.

Ask the student from time to time what *was* said. Curb over- and under-acknowledgment. Let the student do anything at first to get acknowledgment across, then even him out. Teach him that an acknowledgment is a stop, not the beginning of a new cycle of communication or an encouragement to another to go on and that an acknowledgment must be appropriate for the person's communication. The student must not develop the habit of robotically using "Good," "Thank you" as the only acknowledgments.

Another point of this drill is to teach further that one can fail to get an acknowledgment across or can fail to stop a person with an acknowledgment or can take a person's head off with an acknowledgment which is overdone.

Patter: The coach says "Start," reads a line and says "Flunk" every time the coach feels there has been an improper acknowledgment. The coach repeats the same line after each time he says "Flunk." "That's it" may be used to terminate for discussion or terminate the drill session. "Start" must be used to begin again after a "That's it."

This drill is passed only when the student can totally, completely and finally acknowledge a statement, observation or comment in such a way that the person making it is happy with the fact that it has been wholly received and understood and feels no need to repeat it or continue it.

Number: TR 2 1/2

Name: Half-Acknowledgments

A *half-acknowledgment* is a way of keeping a person talking by giving him the feeling that he is being heard.

Purpose: To acquire the skill to encourage someone who is talking to continue talking.

It is not uncommon to communicate with someone who has apparently finished talking but hasn't really completed saying what he intended to say. Consequently, you could acknowledge him before he has completed and end up chopping his communication. In instances such as this, you have to be alert and observe when the person has more to say and not only let the communication flow to its complete end, but encourage the person to continue talking so he can actually complete his communication.

You may, for instance, find yourself in a conversation with someone and want him to continue talking because you want to know more about what he is saying. The use of a half-acknowledgment is a method to encourage this.

Commands: The coach reads lines from *Alice in Wonderland,* omitting "he said's," and the student half-acknowledges the coach in such a way as to cause the coach to continue talking. The coach should give partial statements that would require a half-acknowledgment from the student. The coach repeats any line he feels was not half-acknowledged.

Position: The student and coach are seated facing each other a comfortable distance apart.

Training Stress: Teach the student that a half-acknowledgment is an encouragement to a person to *continue* talking. Curb overacknowledgment that stops a person from talking. Teach him further that a half-acknowledgment is a way of keeping a person talking by giving the person the feeling that he is being heard.

The student nods or gives half-acknowledgments in such a way as to cause the coach to continue talking. The student must not use direct statements such as "go on" or "continue" to accomplish his purpose. Smiling, nodding and other means are employed. The coach must feel persuaded to continue to talk.

Any positive acknowledgments that would end off the communication flow and any failure to look or act in a manner that invites the coach to continue to talk are flunked and the drill is started again.

TR 2 1/2

"In my youth I took to the law..."

COACH   STUDENT

Patter: The coach says "Start," reads a line and says "Flunk" every time the coach feels there has been an improper half-acknowledgment. The coach repeats the same line each time after saying "Flunk," until the student gives a proper half-acknowledgment. "That's it" may be used to terminate for discussion or terminate the drill session. If the drill session is terminated for discussion, the coach must say "Start" again to resume it.

The drill is passed when the student is confident that he can cause at will another person to continue to talk.

"Uh-huh."

COACH   STUDENT

"...and argued each case with my wife."

COACH   STUDENT

Number: TR 3

Name: Getting a Question Answered

Purpose: To acquire the skill of getting a single exact question answered despite diversions.

Have you ever asked a question and not gotten an answer? This can be upsetting, as the communication cycle is incomplete and is left suspended.

In social or other situations, it is important to be able to get your question answered and complete cycles of communication. This drill gives you that ability.

Commands: Either "Do fish swim?" or "Do birds fly?"

Position: Student and coach seated a comfortable distance apart.

Training Stress: One question and student acknowledgment of its answer in one unit of time which is then finished. To keep the student from straying into variations of question.

The student is flunked if he or she fails to get an answer to the question asked, if he or she fails to repeat the exact question, if he or she Q-and-As with excursions taken by the coach.

Q and A is short for "Question and Answer." It means to not get an answer to one's question, to fail to complete something or to deviate from an intended course of action. Example: Question: "Do birds fly?" Answer: "I don't like birds." Question: "Why not?" Answer: "Because they're dirty." This is Q and A—the original question has not been answered and has been dropped and the person who asked the question has deviated. One could say that he "Q-and-Aed."

Each time a question is repeated it exists, theoretically and purely, in its own moment of time and is uttered itself in present time with its own intention.

When a student is being a machine, simply repeating a question over and over again, there is no intention there. Therefore, when one is repeating a question, it must be expressed in present time as itself with its intention. If a question is always uttered in present time it could be said over and over again without any problem. If a question is repeated over and over with no new intention it becomes arduous.

Patter: The coach uses "Start" and "That's it" as in earlier TRs. The coach is not bound after starting to answer the student's question, but may give a commenting-type answer that doesn't really answer the question, in order to throw the student off. Often the coach should answer the actual question asked by the student. Example:

Student: "Do fish swim?"

Coach: "Yes."

Student: "Good."

Somewhat less often the coach attempts to pull the student into a Q and A or upset the student. Example:

Student: "Do fish swim?"

Coach: "Aren't you hungry?"

Student: "Yes."

Coach: "Flunk."

When the question is not answered, the student must repeat the question until he gets an answer. Anything except question and acknowledgment is flunked. Unnecessary repeating of the question is flunked. A poor delivery of the question (e.g., lack of intention) is flunked. A poor acknowledgment is flunked. A Q and A is flunked (as in example). Student upset or confusion is flunked. Student failure to utter the next question without a long communication lag is flunked.

A choppy or premature acknowledgment is flunked. Lack of an acknowledgment (or with a distinct communication lag) is flunked. Any words from the coach except an answer to the question, "Start," "Flunk," "Good" or "That's it" should have no influence on the student except to get him to repeat the question again.

"Start," "Flunk," "Good" and "That's it" may not be used to fluster or trap the student. Any other statement under the sun may be. The coach should not use introverted statements such as, "I just had a realization." "Coach divertive" statements should all concern the student, not the coach, and should be designed to throw the student off and cause the student to lose control or track of what the student is doing. The student's job is to keep the drill going in spite of anything, using only question or acknowledgment. If the student does anything else than the above, it is a flunk and the coach must say so.

When the student can consistently get his question answered despite diversions, he has passed this drill.

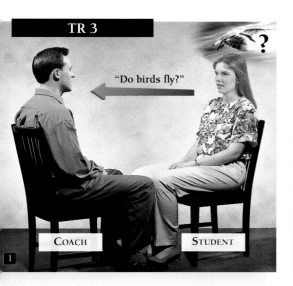

Number: TR 4

Name: Handling Originations

Definition: As used in this drill, the word *origination* means something voluntarily said or done unexpectedly by a person concerning himself, his ideas, reactions or difficulties.

Purpose: To teach the student not to be tongue-tied or startled or thrown off by the originations of another and to maintain good communication throughout an origination.

People frequently say the most astonishing things and take you completely by surprise.

Almost every argument you have had was because you did not handle an origination. If a person walks in and says he just passed with the highest mark in the whole school, and you say how hungry you are, you'll find yourself in a fight. He feels ignored.

Handling an origination merely tells the person you've heard what he said. This might be called a form of acknowledgment, but it isn't; it is the communication formula in reverse. The person you were speaking to is now the cause-point of the communication and is speaking to you. Thus you now have to handle this origination and once again resume your role as cause-point to complete the original communication cycle.

Commands: The student asks the coach, "Do fish swim?" or "Do birds fly?" Coach answers, but now and then makes startling comments from the prepared Origination Sheet provided on page 46. Student must handle originations to satisfaction of coach.

Position: Student and coach sit facing each other at a comfortable distance apart.

Training Stress: The student is taught to hear origination and do three things. (1) Understand it; (2) Acknowledge it; and (3) Return the person to the original cycle of communication so that it can be completed. If the coach feels abruptness or too much time consumed or lack of comprehension, he corrects the student into better handling.

Patter: All originations concern the coach, his ideas, reactions or difficulties, none concern the student. Otherwise the patter is the same as in earlier training routines. The student's patter is governed by: (1) Clarifying and understanding the origination, (2) Acknowledging the origination, (3) Repeating the question. Anything else is a flunk.

The student must be taught to prevent upsets and differentiate between a vital problem that concerns the person and a mere effort to divert him. Flunks are given if the student does more than (1) Understand; (2) Acknowledge; (3) Return the person to the original cycle of communication.

Coach may throw in remarks personal to student as on TR 3. Student's failure to differentiate between these comments (by trying to handle them) and coach's originations about self is a flunk.

Student's failure to persist is always a flunk in any TR but here more so. Coach should not always read from the Origination Sheet to originate, but can make up his own origination, and not always look at student when about to comment. By *originate* is meant to make a statement or remark referring to the state of the coach or his fancied worries, feelings, attitudes, etc. By *comment* is meant a statement or remark aimed only at student or room. Originations are handled, comments are disregarded by the student. Example:

Student: "Do birds fly?"

Coach: "Yes."

Student: "Thank you."

Student: "Do birds fly?"

Coach: "I went fishing yesterday."

Student: "Thanks for letting me know. Do birds fly?"

Coach: "Yes, they do."

Student: "Very good."

When the student can smoothly handle originations without being startled or thrown off and can maintain good communication throughout an origination, he has passed this drill.

COACHING

Coaching is a technology in itself, a vital part of Scientology study. It should be thoroughly understood by both you and your partner before starting to drill any of the TRs.

Good coaching can make the difference between getting through a drill with excellent results for a student or not getting through the drill at all.

In order to help you to do the best you possibly can as far as being a coach is concerned, below you will find a few data that will assist you:

1. *Coach with a purpose.*

Have for your goal when you are coaching someone that the student is going to get the training drill correct; be purposeful in working toward obtaining this goal. Whenever you correct the student as a coach, just don't do it with no reason, with no purpose. Have the purpose in mind for the student to get a better understanding of the training drill and to do it to the best of his ability.

2. *Coach with reality.*

Be realistic in your coaching. When you give an origination to a student, really make it an origination, not just something that the sheet said you should say, so that it is as if the student was having to handle it exactly as you say under real conditions and circumstances. This does not mean, however, that you really feel the things that you are giving the student, such as saying to him, "My leg hurts." This does not mean that your leg should hurt, but you should say it in such a manner as to get across to the student that your leg hurts. Another thing about this is do not use any experiences from your past to coach with. Be inventive in the present.

3. *Coach with an intention.*

Behind all your coaching should be your intention that by the end of the drill the student will be aware that he is doing better at the end of it than he did at the beginning. The student must have a feeling that he has accomplished something in the training drill, no matter how small it is. It is your intention and always should be while coaching that the student you are coaching be a more able person and have a greater understanding of that on which he is being coached.

4. *In coaching take up only one thing at a time.*

For example, using TR 4, if the student arrives at the goal set up for TR 4, then check over, one at a time, the earlier TRs. Is he confronting you? Does he originate the question to you each time as his own and did he really intend for you to receive it? Are his acknowledgments ending the cycles of communication, etc. But only coach these things one at a time, never two or more at a time. Make sure that the student does each thing you coach him on correctly before going on to the next training step. The better a student gets at a particular drill or a particular part of a drill you should demand, as a coach, a higher standard of ability. This does not mean that you should be "never satisfied." It does mean that a person can always get better, and once you have reached a certain level of ability, then work toward a new plateau.

If you do find that the student is having a hard time on one of the drills, the first thing to do is have him read over the text of the drill and find any words he did not fully understand and look them up in a dictionary. If this does not remedy the situation, check if it is one of the *earlier* drills that he is hung up on. If you find this to be the case, you should go back to the earlier one he is hung up on and get him through that drill to a pass. Once you have done that, start on the next drill and do that one to a pass and come up again through the later ones.

As a coach, you should always work in the direction of better and more precise coaching. Never allow yourself to do a sloppy job of coaching because you would be doing your student a disservice, and we doubt that you would like the same disservice when you are the one being a student.

In coaching, never give an opinion as such, but always give your directions as a direct statement, rather than saying, "I think" or "Well, maybe it might be this way," etc.

When a coach, you are primarily responsible for the drill and the results that are obtained on the student.

Once in a while the student will start to rationalize and justify what he is doing if he is doing something wrong. He will give you reasons why and "becauses." Talking about such things at great length does not accomplish very much. The only thing that does accomplish the goals of the TR and resolves any differences is doing the drill. You will get further by doing it than by talking about it.

In the TRs, the coach should coach with the material given under "Training Stress" and "Purpose."

These drills occasionally have a tendency to upset the student. There is a possibility that during a drill a student may become angry or upset. Should this occur, the coach must help the student through the upset rather than ending the drill and leaving the student in distress. In such an instance, just leaving the student sitting there will in fact leave him more upset than getting him through the drill. The intention of the drill is to teach the student to communicate, and any upset is purely incidental to the drill and plays no part in it.

There is a small thing that most people forget to do and that is telling the student when he has gotten the drill right or he has done a good job on a particular step. Besides correcting wrongnesses, there is also complimenting rightness.

You very definitely "flunk" the student for anything that amounts to "self-coaching" (where the student attempts to correct himself). The reason for this is that the student will tend to introvert (look inward) and will look too much at how he is doing and what he is doing rather than just doing it.

As a coach, keep your attention on the student and how he is doing and don't become so interested in what you yourself are doing that you neglect the student and are unaware of his ability or inability to do the drill correctly. It is easy to become "interesting" to a student, to make him laugh and act up a bit. But your main job as a coach is to see how good he can get in each training drill and that is what you should have your attention on; that, and how well he is doing.

To a large degree the progress of the student is determined by the standard of coaching. Good results produce better people.

Once coaching is understood by you and your partner, you are ready to drill on the TRs. Doing these drills exactly as described is key to successfully mastering them.

It takes hours and hours of practice on these drills to perfect them, but it is time well spent. Each of the TRs is done until the student has achieved the purpose of the drill and can *do* that TR.

A student can spend many hours on any TR before reaching a point where he really acquires the skill of that TR and maintains it. This is particularly true of *TR 0 Be There, TR 0 Confronting* and *TR 0 Bullbait.*

There is one TR which has a specific time requirement for passing: on *TR 0 Confronting,* the student is to do the drill until he has reached a point where he can do it comfortably for two hours straight.

The coach works with the student on a particular TR to a point where the student achieves an increased ability to do the drill well. However, it is better to go through the TRs several times, from *TR 0 Be There* to *TR 4* in sequence, getting tougher each time, than to stay on one forever or for the coach to be so tough at the start that the student goes into a decline.

With tough but fair coaching conducted on a proper gradient, the student will complete these TRs with certainty in his ability to apply the communication formula in any situation he may be called upon to face.

This is one of the most valuable abilities he will ever learn.

Origination Sheet

Coach uses these now and then in Training Routine Number 4
Handling Originations

I have a pain in my stomach.

The room seems bigger.

My body feels heavy.

I had a twitch in my leg.

I feel like I'm sinking.

The colors in the room are brighter.

My head feels lopsided.

I feel wonderful.

I have an awful feeling of fear.

You are the first person who ever listened to me.

I just realized I've had a headache for years.

This is silly.

I feel all confused.

I've got a sharp pain in my back.

I feel lighter somehow.

I can't tell you.

I feel terrible—like I'd lost something, or something.

WOW—I didn't know that before.

The room seems to be getting dark.

I feel awfully tense.

You surely have a nice office here.

I feel warm all over.

By the way, I won that tennis tournament yesterday.

My head feels like it has a tight band round it. *Continued...*

When are you going to get a haircut?

I feel like I was all hemmed in somehow.

Who is going to win the cup final?

This chair is so comfortable I could go to sleep.

I keep thinking about that cop who blew his whistle at me
    this morning.

How long do we have to do this?

My face tingles.

I'm getting sleepy.

I'm starving. Let's go to lunch.

Suddenly, I'm so tired.

Everything is getting blurry.

Is this room rocking?

I just realized how wrong I've been all my life.

I feel like there is a spider's web on my face.

My left knee hurts.

I feel so light!

Isn't it getting hotter in here?

I just remembered the first time I went swimming.

My back has been aching like this for years.

Are you married?

I feel so lonesome.

I feel like I can't talk.

My body is starting to shake all over.

My ribs hurt.

Everything seems to be getting dark.

Don't you get tired of listening to someone like me?

COMMUNICATION IS LIFE

One's ability to communicate can spell the difference between success or failure in all aspects of living. You will notice that those people you know who are successful in their endeavors generally have a high ability to communicate; those who are not, do not.

Communication is not just a way of getting along in life, it is the heart of life. It is by thousands of percent the senior factor in understanding life and living it successfully.

We instinctively revere the great artist, painter or musician, and society as a whole looks upon them as not quite ordinary beings. And they are not. But the understanding and skilled use of communication is not only for the artist, it is for anyone.

In examining the whole subject of communication, one is apt to discover, if he takes a penetrating look, that there are very few people around him who are actually *communicating,* but that there are a lot of people who think they are communicating who are not.

The apparency sometimes is that it is better not to communicate than to communicate, but that is never really the case. Communication is the solvent for any human problem. An understanding of communication itself was not available before Scientology.

A thorough knowledge of the communication formula and an understanding of how any difficulties in its application can be recognized and corrected are vital tools to successful living. The knowledge and drills contained in this booklet will start one on the road to success. A professional level of skill can be attained in Scientology churches on the Hubbard Professional TR Course. Here, expert supervision and complete data on the subject are available to those wishing to perfect their ability to communicate.

Communication is life.

Without it we are dead to all.

To the degree we can communicate, we are alive. ■

PRACTICAL EXERCISES

Here are exercises relating to communication. Doing these exercises will help increase your understanding of the knowledge contained in this booklet.

1 Look around and observe examples of the different parts of communication; note which parts are used and not used in conversations you observe (including intention, attention, duplication, understanding, and whether the people involved are factually being source-point or receipt-point). Continue to observe communications around you until you can easily identify the various parts of communication and identify any parts which are absent or not being used correctly.

2 Notice acknowledgments in communication. Observe two people talking, and pay particular attention to the use of acknowledgment by each person. Note any lack of acknowledgment as well. What differences do you observe in communication when acknowledgment is present compared to when it is not present?

3 Observe two-way communication between two people. Note whether the communication is smooth or not, and observe the different elements of good communication or their absence. Observe other two-way communication cycles, repeating this same exercise.

4 Do each of the TRs. Work with another person as your partner and do the drills, beginning with *TR 0 Be There*. Do each drill exactly as stated in the booklet with the proper use of coaching, until you and your partner both complete each drill to a pass.

RESULTS FROM APPLICATION

The success level of a person is directly linked to his communication level. People who understand the basics of good communication make others around them feel comfortable, understood and recognized. In short, they make others feel worthwhile and important.

The stories below bear testimony to the fact that a person is as alive as he can communicate, and that communication is the universal solvent.

In Europe, a mother had been having great difficulty communicating with her sixteen-year-old daughter. Their relationship became even more strained when she discovered that her daughter had been taking drugs. Here is what she had to say about a Scientology communication course they participated in together as part of a drug withdrawal program:

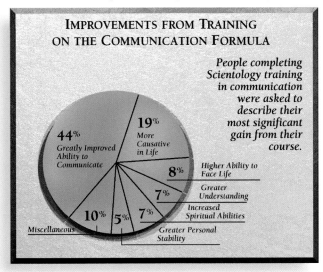

IMPROVEMENTS FROM TRAINING ON THE COMMUNICATION FORMULA

People completing Scientology training in communication were asked to describe their most significant gain from their course.

44% Greatly Improved Ability to Communicate

19% More Causative in Life

8% Higher Ability to Face Life

7% Greater Understanding

7% Increased Spiritual Abilities

5% Greater Personal Stability

10% Miscellaneous

"This course only took a few hours a day. At that time my daughter and I were not really talking with each other. It was mostly just 'hellos' and 'goodbyes.' The communication course not only helped us to begin to communicate again, but taught us some very valuable things about communicating with another person. We learned how to be relaxed around other people, how to effectively talk as well as listen, how to confront our problems and problems in general, and not run away. The things we learned in those few hours will stay with us a lifetime."

A volunteer nurse in South Africa was traveling in a taxi with several other people when they were held up by an angry man brandishing a knife. At that moment she asked herself, "What data could I apply now that I learned in the Scientology workshops I attended?" She had learned about communication, and determined that all she had to do was face the man *and* the situation and use her communication skills. She then proceeded to quietly talk to the man, telling him not to do something that he would later regret, just for the sake of a little money. This made sense to the criminal and he gave the money back to everyone in the taxi. She was proud that she had been able to handle the situation by using the communication skills she acquired in the Scientology workshops.

Being extremely depressed, a young man from Hawaii was literally looking for a high building to jump from. Luckily, he didn't find one high enough before a friend advised him to instead take a course in Scientology on communication. He went ahead and did the course, despite being barely literate. As he put it:

*"I went from someone who wanted to be a nail to someone who is a hammer. It **totally** changed my life! My friends could not believe the miraculous change in me."*

Growing up as a teenager was very difficult for a young woman from Los Angeles as she was not able to communicate to her parents as she would have liked to. She related:

"I loved my parents, but sometimes my communication would not get across to them. I, of course, blamed them for this. After learning the communication formula, and learning what two-way communication was, I was very surprised to find that it was quite easy to talk to my parents. We can now talk about most anything and there is understanding between us, where there wasn't before. The love between us has grown and I like it very much. What a difference this has made in my life. Thank you, Mr. Hubbard."

In New York City, a girl who had just learned about L. Ron Hubbard's technology on communication was walking home with her husband one night when they heard sudden screeching brakes and a thump. They swiftly walked over to the scene of the accident—a man had been hit by a car driven by a drunk driver. The wife said that just by knowing and using the communication formula and how to control a situation, she was able to handle a lot of confusion:

"The man was obviously in pain. My husband immediately began using basic Scientology techniques to assist the man and told me to start putting order into the environment. So I got the drunken driver and the other four unruly, intoxicated men out of their car and got them under control. By then a crowd of nearly fifty people had gathered and within ten minutes, using what I had learned about communication, I had them under control too. When the police showed up, there was virtually nothing left for them to do. I told one of them what we had done and then another cop, who hadn't heard our communication cycle, asked me to step behind the rope. The cop I had spoken to told him, 'Not her, she's the one that did our job!' The driver was carted off to jail and the man who was hit was doing much better on his way to the hospital. We were taken to the police station and filed reports as witnesses and were thanked by the New York Police Department. The sergeant told us that he wished a lot more people could do what we did. This stuff works!"

GLOSSARY

acknowledge: give (someone) an acknowledgment. *See also* **acknowledgment** in this glossary.

acknowledgment: something said or done to inform another that his statement or action has been noted, understood and received.

affinity: love, liking or any other emotional attitude; the degree of liking. The basic definition of affinity is the consideration of distance, whether good or bad.

bullbait: to find certain actions, words, phrases, mannerisms or subjects that cause the student doing a drill to become distracted by reacting to the coach. *Bullbaiting* is done by the coach in specific Training Routines. The word *bullbait* is derived from an English and Spanish sport of *baiting* which meant to set dogs upon a chained bull. *See also* **Training Routines** in this glossary.

button: an item, word, phrase, subject or area that causes response or reaction in an individual.

communication: an interchange of ideas across space between two individuals.

communication lag: the length of time intervening between the asking of a question and the reply to that specific question by the person asked.

confront: to face without flinching or avoiding. The ability to confront is actually the ability to be there comfortably and perceive.

cycle of action: the sequence that an action goes through, wherein the action is begun, is continued for as long as is required and then is completed as planned.

Dianetics: comes from the Greek words *dia,* meaning "through" and *nous,* meaning "soul." Dianetics is a methodology developed by L. Ron Hubbard which can help alleviate such ailments as unwanted sensations and emotions, irrational fears and psychosomatic illnesses. It is most accurately described as *what the soul is doing to the body through the mind.*

drill: a method of learning or training whereby a person does a procedure over and over again in order to perfect that skill.

duplication: the act of reproducing something exactly.

gradient: a gradual approach to something taken step by step, level by level, each step or level being, of itself, easily attainable—so that finally, complicated and difficult activities can be achieved with relative ease. The term *gradient* also applies to each of the steps taken in such an approach.

major stable win: *See* **win** in this glossary.

present time: the time which is now and becomes the past as rapidly as it is observed. It is a term loosely applied to the environment existing in now.

Q and A: short for *Question and Answer.* It means to not get an answer to one's question, to fail to complete something or to deviate from an intended course of action. Example: Question: "Do birds fly?" Answer: "I don't like birds." Question: "Why not?" Answer: "Because they're dirty." The original question has not been answered and has been dropped and the person who asked the question has deviated—this is Q and A. The person who deviates could be said to have "Q-and-Aed."

reality: that which appears to be. Reality is fundamentally agreement; the degree of agreement reached by people. What we agree to be real is real.

Scientology: an applied religious philosophy developed by L. Ron Hubbard. It is the study and handling of the spirit in relationship to itself, universes and other life. The word *Scientology* comes from the Latin *scio,* which means "know" and the Greek word *logos,* meaning "the word or outward form by which the inward thought is expressed and made known." Thus, Scientology means knowing about knowing.

terminal: a person, point or position which can receive, relay or send a communication.

TR: abbreviation for *Training Routine. See* **Training Routines** in this glossary.

Training Routines: training drills that enable a person to improve his level of communication skill. By doing these drills any person's ability to communicate with others can be vastly improved.

win: the accomplishment of any desired improvement. Examples of wins would be a person increasing his ability to communicate, experiencing an increased feeling of well-being or gaining more certainty about some area of his life. In Training Routines, when a student has reached the point where he can do a drill and his skill and ability to do it is stable, it is called a major stable win—a significant, lasting gain. *See also* **Training Routines** in this glossary.

ABOUT L. RON HUBBARD

Born in Tilden, Nebraska on March 13, 1911, his road of discovery and dedication to his fellows began at an early age. By the age of nineteen, he had traveled more than a quarter of a million miles, examining the cultures of Java, Japan, India and the Philippines.

Returning to the United States in 1929, Ron resumed his formal education and studied mathematics, engineering and the then new field of nuclear physics—all providing vital tools for continued research. To finance that research, Ron embarked upon a literary career in the early 1930s, and soon became one of the most widely read authors of popular fiction. Yet never losing sight of his primary goal, he continued his mainline research through extensive travel and expeditions.

With the advent of World War II, he entered the United States Navy as a lieutenant (junior grade) and served as commander of antisubmarine corvettes. Left partially blind and lame from injuries sustained during combat, he was diagnosed as permanently disabled by 1945. Through application of his theories on the mind, however, he was not only able to help fellow servicemen, but also to regain his own health.

After five more years of intensive research, Ron's discoveries were presented to the world in *Dianetics: The Modern Science of Mental Health*. The first popular handbook on the human mind expressly written for the man in the street, *Dianetics* ushered in a new era of hope for mankind and a new phase of life for its author. He did, however, not cease his research, and as breakthrough after breakthrough was carefully codified through late 1951, the applied religious philosophy of Scientology was born.

Because Scientology explains the whole of life, there is no aspect of man's existence that L. Ron Hubbard's subsequent work did not address. Residing variously in the United States and England, his continued research brought forth solutions to such social ills as declining educational standards and pandemic drug abuse.

All told, L. Ron Hubbard's works on Scientology and Dianetics total forty million words of recorded lectures, books and writings. Together, these constitute the legacy of a lifetime that ended on January 24, 1986. Yet the passing of L. Ron Hubbard in no way constituted an end; for with a hundred million of his books in circulation and millions of people daily applying his technologies for betterment, it can truly be said the world still has no greater friend.■

CHURCHES OF SCIENTOLOGY
Contact Your Nearest Church or Organization
or visit www.volunteerministers.org

UNITED STATES

ALBUQUERQUE
Church of Scientology
8106 Menaul Boulevard NE
Albuquerque, New Mexico
87110

ANN ARBOR
Church of Scientology
66 E. Michigan Avenue
Battle Creek, Michigan 49017

ATLANTA
Church of Scientology
1611 Mt. Vernon Road
Dunwoody, Georgia 30338

AUSTIN
Church of Scientology
2200 Guadalupe
Austin, Texas 78705

BOSTON
Church of Scientology
448 Beacon Street
Boston, Massachusetts 02115

BUFFALO
Church of Scientology
836 N. Main Street
Buffalo, New York 14202

CHICAGO
Church of Scientology
3011 North Lincoln Avenue
Chicago, Illinois 60657-4207

CINCINNATI
Church of Scientology
215 West 4th Street, 5th Floor
Cincinnati, Ohio 45202-2670

CLEARWATER
Church of Scientology
Flag Service Organization
210 South Fort Harrison Avenue
Clearwater, Florida 33756

Foundation Church of
Scientology
Flag Ship Service Organization
c/o *Freewinds* Relay Office
118 North Fort Harrison Avenue
Clearwater, Florida 33755-4013

COLUMBUS
Church of Scientology
30 North High Street
Columbus, Ohio 43215

DALLAS
Church of Scientology
Celebrity Centre Dallas
1850 North Buckner Boulevard
Dallas, Texas 75228

DENVER
Church of Scientology
3385 South Bannock Street
Englewood, Colorado 80110

DETROIT
Church of Scientology
28000 Middlebelt Road
Farmington Hills, Michigan
48334

HONOLULU
Church of Scientology
1146 Bethel Street
Honolulu, Hawaii 96813

KANSAS CITY
Church of Scientology
3619 Broadway
Kansas City, Missouri 64111

LAS VEGAS
Church of Scientology
846 East Sahara Avenue
Las Vegas, Nevada 89104

Church of Scientology
Celebrity Centre Las Vegas
4850 W. Flamingo Road, Suite 10
Las Vegas, Nevada 89103

LONG ISLAND
Church of Scientology
64 Bethpage Road
Hicksville, New York
11801-2850

LOS ANGELES AND
VICINITY
Church of Scientology
of Los Angeles
4810 Sunset Boulevard
Los Angeles, California 90027

Church of Scientology
1451 Irvine Boulevard
Tustin, California 92680

Church of Scientology
1277 East Colorado Boulevard
Pasadena, California 91106

Church of Scientology
15643 Sherman Way
Van Nuys, California 91406

Church of Scientology
American Saint Hill
Organization
1413 L. Ron Hubbard Way
Los Angeles, California 90027

Church of Scientology
American Saint Hill Foundation
1413 L. Ron Hubbard Way
Los Angeles, California 90027

Church of Scientology
Advanced Organization
of Los Angeles
1306 L. Ron Hubbard Way
Los Angeles, California 90027

Church of Scientology
Celebrity Centre International
5930 Franklin Avenue
Hollywood, California 90028

LOS GATOS
Church of Scientology
650 Saratoga Avenue,
San Jose, California 95117

MIAMI
Church of Scientology
120 Giralda Avenue
Coral Gables, Florida 33134

MINNEAPOLIS
Church of Scientology
Twin Cities
1011 Nicollet Mall
Minneapolis, Minnesota 55403

MOUNTAIN VIEW
Church of Scientology
2483 Old Middlefield Way
Mountain View, California
94043

NASHVILLE
Church of Scientology
Celebrity Centre Nashville
1204 16th Avenue South
Nashville, Tennessee 37212

NEW HAVEN
Church of Scientology
909 Whalley Avenue
New Haven, Connecticut
06515-1728

NEW YORK CITY
Church of Scientology
227 West 46th Street
New York, New York
10036-1409

Church of Scientology
Celebrity Centre New York
65 East 82nd Street
New York, New York 10028

ORLANDO
Church of Scientology
1830 East Colonial Drive
Orlando, Florida 32803-4729

PHILADELPHIA
Church of Scientology
1315 Race Street
Philadelphia, Pennsylvania
19107

PHOENIX
Church of Scientology
2702 N. 44th St., Suite A100
Phoenix, Arizona 85038

PORTLAND
Church of Scientology
2636 NE Sandy Boulevard
Portland, Oregon 97232-2342

Church of Scientology
Celebrity Centre Portland
708 SW Salmon Street
Portland, Oregon 97205

SACRAMENTO
Church of Scientology
825 15th Street
Sacramento, California
95814-2096

SALT LAKE CITY
Church of Scientology
1931 South 1100 East
Salt Lake City, Utah 84106

SAN DIEGO
Church of Scientology
1330 4th Avenue
San Diego, California 92101

SAN FRANCISCO
Church of Scientology
701 Montgomery Street
San Francisco, California 94111

SAN JOSE
Church of Scientology
80 East Rosemary Street
San Jose, California 95112

SANTA BARBARA
Church of Scientology
524 State Street
Santa Barbara, California 93101

SEATTLE
Church of Scientology
2226 3rd Avenue
Seattle, Washington 98121

ST. LOUIS
Church of Scientology
6901 Delmar Boulevard
University City, Missouri 63130

TAMPA
Church of Scientology
3102 N. Havana Avenue
Tampa, Florida 33607

WASHINGTON, DC
Founding Church of Scientology
of Washington, DC
1701 20th Street NW
Washington, DC 20009

PUERTO RICO

HATO REY
Dianetics Center of Puerto Rico
272 JT Piñero Avenue
Hyde Park
San Juan, Puerto Rico 00918

CANADA

EDMONTON
Church of Scientology
10206 106th Street NW
Edmonton, Alberta
Canada T5J 1H7

KITCHENER
Church of Scientology
104 King Street West, 2nd Floor
Kitchener, Ontario
Canada N2G 1A6

MONTREAL
Church of Scientology
4489 Papineau Street
Montreal, Quebec
Canada H2H 1T7

OTTAWA
Church of Scientology
150 Rideau Street, 2nd Floor
Ottawa, Ontario
Canada K1N 5X6

QUEBEC
Church of Scientology
350 Bd Chareste Est
Quebec, Quebec
Canada G1K 3H5

TORONTO
Church of Scientology
696 Yonge Street, 2nd Floor
Toronto, Ontario
Canada M4Y 2A7

VANCOUVER
Church of Scientology
401 West Hastings Street
Vancouver, British Columbia
Canada V6B 1L5

WINNIPEG
Church of Scientology
315 Garry Street, Suite 210
Winnipeg, Manitoba
Canada R3B 2G7

UNITED KINGDOM

BIRMINGHAM
Church of Scientology
8 Ethel Street
Winston Churchill House
Birmingham, England B2 4BG

BRIGHTON
Church of Scientology
Third Floor, 79-83 North Street
Brighton, Sussex
England BN1 1ZA

EAST GRINSTEAD
Church of Scientology
Saint Hill Foundation
Saint Hill Manor
East Grinstead, West Sussex
England RH19 4JY

Advanced Organization
Saint Hill
Saint Hill Manor
East Grinstead, West Sussex
England RH19 4JY

EDINBURGH
Hubbard Academy of Personal
Independence
20 Southbridge
Edinburgh, Scotland EH1 1LL

LONDON
Church of Scientology
68 Tottenham Court Road
London, England W1P 0BB

Church of Scientology
Celebrity Centre London
42 Leinster Gardens
London, England W2 3AN

MANCHESTER
Church of Scientology
258 Deansgate
Manchester, England M3 4BG

PLYMOUTH
Church of Scientology
41 Ebrington Street
Plymouth, Devon
England PL4 9AA

SUNDERLAND
Church of Scientology
51 Fawcett Street
Sunderland, Tyne and Wear
England SR1 1RS

AUSTRALIA

ADELAIDE
Church of Scientology
24–28 Waymouth Street
Adelaide, South Australia
Australia 5000

BRISBANE
Church of Scientology
106 Edward Street, 2nd Floor
Brisbane, Queensland
Australia 4000

CANBERRA
Church of Scientology
43–45 East Row
Canberra City, ACT
Australia 2601

MELBOURNE
Church of Scientology
42–44 Russell Street
Melbourne, Victoria
Australia 3000

PERTH
Church of Scientology
108 Murray Street, 1st Floor
Perth, Western Australia
Australia 6000

SYDNEY
Church of Scientology
201 Castlereagh Street
Sydney, New South Wales
Australia 2000

Church of Scientology
Advanced Organization
Saint Hill Australia,
New Zealand and Oceania
19–37 Greek Street
Glebe, New South Wales
Australia 2037

NEW ZEALAND

AUCKLAND
Church of Scientology
159 Queen Street, 3rd Floor
Auckland 1, New Zealand

AFRICA

BULAWAYO
Church of Scientology
Southampton House, Suite 202
Main Street and 9th Avenue
Bulawayo, Zimbabwe

CAPE TOWN
Church of Scientology
Ground Floor, Dorlane House
39 Roeland Street
Cape Town 8001, South Africa

DURBAN
Church of Scientology
20 Buckingham Terrace
Westville, Durban 3630
South Africa

HARARE
Church of Scientology
404-409 Pockets Building
50 Jason Moyo Avenue
Harare, Zimbabwe

JOHANNESBURG
Church of Scientology
4th Floor, Budget House
130 Main Street
Johannesburg 2001
South Africa

Church of Scientology
No. 108 1st Floor,
Bordeaux Centre
Gordon Road, Corner Jan
Smuts Avenue
Blairgowrie, Randburg 2125
South Africa

PORT ELIZABETH
Church of Scientology
2 St. Christopher's
27 Westbourne Road Central
Port Elizabeth 6001
South Africa

PRETORIA
Church of Scientology
307 Ancore Building
Corner Jeppe and Esselen Streets
Sunnyside, Pretoria 0002
South Africa

SCIENTOLOGY MISSIONS

INTERNATIONAL OFFICE
Scientology Missions
International
6331 Hollywood Boulevard
Suite 501
Los Angeles, California
90028-6314

UNITED STATES
Scientology Missions
International
Western United States Office
1308 L. Ron Hubbard Way
Los Angeles, California 90027

Scientology Missions
International
Eastern United States Office
349 W. 48th Street
New York, New York 10036

Scientology Missions
International
Flag Land Base Office
210 South Fort Harrison Avenue
Clearwater, Florida 33756

AFRICA
Scientology Missions
International
African Office
6th Floor, Budget House
130 Main Street
Johannesburg 2001
South Africa

AUSTRALIA, NEW ZEALAND AND OCEANIA
Scientology Missions
International
Australian, New Zealand
and Oceanian Office
201 Castlereagh Street, 3rd Flr.
Sydney, New South Wales
Australia 2000

CANADA
Scientology Missions
International
Canadian Office
696 Yonge Street
Toronto, Ontario
Canada M4Y 2A7

UNITED KINGDOM
Scientology Missions
International
United Kingdom Office
Saint Hill Manor
East Grinstead, West Sussex
England RH19 4JY

TO OBTAIN ANY BOOKS OR CAS-
SETTES BY L. RON HUBBARD WHICH
ARE NOT AVAILABLE AT YOUR LOCAL
ORGANIZATION, CONTACT ANY OF
THE FOLLOWING PUBLICATIONS
ORGANIZATIONS WORLDWIDE:

BRIDGE PUBLICATIONS, INC.
4751 Fountain Avenue
Los Angeles, California 90029
www.bridgepub.com

**NEW ERA PUBLICATIONS
INTERNATIONAL ApS**
Store Kongensgade 53
1264 Copenhagen K
Denmark
www.newerapublications.com

BUILD A BETTER WORLD

BECOME A VOLUNTEER MINISTER

Help bring happiness, purpose and truth to your fellow man.
Become a Volunteer Minister.

Thousands of Volunteer Ministers bring relief and sanity to others all over the world using techniques like the ones found in this booklet. But more help is needed. Your help. As a Volunteer Minister you can today handle things which seemed impossible yesterday. And you can vastly improve this world's tomorrow.

Become a Volunteer Minister and brighten the world to a better place for you to live. It's easy to do. For help and information about becoming a Volunteer Minister, visit our website today. www.volunteerministers.org

You can also call or write your nearest Volunteer Ministers International organization.

VOLUNTEER MINISTERS INTERNATIONAL
A DEPARTMENT OF THE INTERNATIONAL HUBBARD ECCLESIASTICAL LEAGUE OF PASTORS

INTERNATIONAL OFFICE
6331 Hollywood Boulevard, Suite 708
Los Angeles, California 90028
Tel: (323) 960-3560 (800) 435-7498

WESTERN US
1308 L. Ron Hubbard Way
Los Angeles, California 90027
Tel: (323) 953-3357
1-888-443-5760
ihelpwestus@earthlink.net

EASTERN US
349 W. 48th Street
New York, New York 10036
Tel: (212) 757-9610
1-888-443-5788

CANADA
696 Yonge Street
Toronto, Ontario
Canada M4Y 2A7
Tel: (416) 968-0070

LATIN AMERICA
Federación Mexicana de
  Dianética, A.C.
Puebla #31
Colonia Roma, CP 06700
Mexico, D.F.
Tel: 525-511-4452

EUROPE
Store Kongensgade 55
1264 Copenhagen K
Denmark
Tel: 45-33-737-322

ITALY
Via Cadorna, 61
20090 Vimodrone (MI)
Italy
Tel: 39-0227-409-246

AUSTRALIA
201 Castlereagh Street
3rd Floor
Sydney, New South Wales
Australia 2000
Tel: 612-9267-6422

AFRICA
6th Floor, Budget House
130 Main Street
Johannesburg 2001
South Africa
Tel: 083-331-7170

UNITED KINGDOM
Saint Hill Manor
East Grinstead, West Sussex
England RH19 4JY
Tel: 44-1342-301-895

HUNGARY
1438 Budapest
PO Box 351, Hungary
Tel: 361-321-5298

COMMONWEALTH OF INDEPENDENT STATES
c/o Hubbard Humanitarian
  Center
Ul. Borisa Galushkina 19A
129301 Moscow, Russia
Tel: 7-095-961-3414

TAIWAN
2F, 65, Sec. 4
Ming-Sheng East Road
Taipei, Taiwan ROC
Tel: 88-628-770-5074

www.volunteerministers.org

Bridge Publications, Inc.
4751 Fountain Avenue, Los Angeles, California 90029
ISBN 0-88404-912-4

Printed in the United States

An L. RON HUBBARD Publication